BEAUTIFUL MUTANTS

beautiful mutants

ADAM POTTLE

CAITLIN PRESS

HALFMOON BAY · BRITISH COLUMBIA

Caitlin Press Inc.
8100 Alderwood Road,
Halfmoon Bay, BC V0N 1Y1
www.caitlin-press.com

Edited by Joe Denham.
Text design by Rachel Page.
Cover design by Vici Johnstone.
Cover image by Laura Ferguson.
Author photo by Kristen Hergott.
Artist photo by Ehud Azoulai.
Printed in Canada

Caitlin Press Inc. acknowledges financial support from the Government of Canada
through the Canada Book Fund and the Canada Council for the Arts, and from the
Province of British Columbia through the British Columbia Arts Council and the
Book Publisher's Tax Credit.

Library and Archives Canada Cataloguing in Publication

Pottle, Adam
Beautiful mutants / Adam Pottle.

Poems.
ISBN 978-1-894759-59-5

I. Title.

PS8631.O7746B42 2011   C811'.6   C2011-901960-4

TABLE OF CONTENTS

For my family

For Debbie

For beautiful mutants everywhere

LOOSENING CIRCLES

THE SPIDER

When I was a kid, I'd pick up a spider
and one by one pull off its legs.

It would always be in a jar with other spiders,
crawling over them and along the leaves I put inside,
dragging its webs over the papery rinds. When I opened
the jar, a damp heat swelled up. The heat of toil. Spider breath.

I chose the biggest, strongest one. I pulled it out
of the jar and held it up by one leg,
its other legs pawing desperately
at my fingertips, its tiny fangs straining. I held it
in such a way that it dangled and had no means of escape.

The spider shuddered when I pulled off its legs.
It curled up and seemed to plead with me. I kept plucking
and eventually tossed its legs into the grass.

I took the spider, now just a face and a belly, and set it back
in its jar. The others, waiting beneath the leaves, encircled
the stubbly brown orb. It bit at the predators. The pinched eyes
shifted, the twiggy jaws swiped, and the dried leaves tipped.
The others soon backed away. I watched for what seemed
like hours, until the little body tired and rolled over, and the others
swarmed, and I went back in the house, silent, in awe.

VIEW FROM A SASKATCHEWAN COUNTRY HOSPITAL ROOM

He stands at the window. It's April. Grey. The field's flat,
patchy with spring stubble. Some kind of crop. He doesn't know.
He chews on a hangnail. In the distance a falcon hovers, circling
around something on the ground. Behind him his daughter lies on the bed,
nearly comatose with pain and medication. Her legs and trunk thick with bandages.
Eyes soldered shut with bruises. He keeps thinking, She's only eleven.
As though there's a right age for this sort of thing. When he looks
at her he hears the metal shrieking, the bones skidding, the vertebrae
shifting. How do nerves sound when they break? Cables snapping.
She'll need diapers now. Feels like last week she just got out of them.
They used to joke. When she was a toddler she once got into
the diaper pail and put a soiled diaper in her mouth. Will they
joke now? He bites down. Tears off the hangnail.

The falcon's gyre widens, loosens. He can't see its target; ground
as grey and indistinct as the day. He forces up a sliver of blood
from the hangnail. Wonders how he'll comfort her. Squints
through his daughter's reflection in the window, trying to focus
on the falcon's target. Thinks he sees something brown
but the grey overtakes it. He looks for her eyes in the glass. Sighs
and glances at her over his shoulder. Her eyes clench, relax.
When he looks outside again the falcon's gone. Nothing moves
in the field. He searches in vain before he turns
and sits down beside her, staring at her blackened eyes.

Mary Kept Immaculate

I was talking to this woman named Mary who back in the sixties had been a trainee at the Alberta Provincial Training School for Mental Defectives in Red Deer, even though she scored normal on one of the IQ tests. I asked her what the people were like and what the rules were and how she was treated. She said, At first it was fine, we all got along so well. The staff helped us through some difficult things and we all worked hard, in the wards and on the pasture, where the cows were kept. But then this man named le Vann came, and things changed. How, I asked. He was very strict and he made everyone else around him strict. The stripes on the bedsheets on all the beds in the ward had to be perfectly lined up, one bed to the next, all the way down the row. Also, he would threaten us with sterilization if we made fun or disobeyed. It was when we the girls began to menstruate that he and the administration really paid attention. They said, We can't have blood (or anything else) running loose in a girl's body or in a girl's head. I wanted to say that the boys were just as bad, if not worse. Anyways, Mary said. And then, I asked. And then it happened, she said. They've shut the school down now, but I remember it all so clearly. I can still hear the little girls, the ones who skipped past on the sidewalk outside, singing about us. And after that, I was let go. I remember how cool it felt. How strange. It felt so strange being outside without having to go back in. And then forty years of this uncertainty, like somebody's taken a piece of me and has been controlling me through that one piece.

Red Deer Skip-rope Rhyme

Harriet's gone, and Lacey too,
behind the walls of the stupid-school!
Mommies and daddies all hate fools—
so don't fail math, 'cause you'll go, too!

The Difference between Normal and Moron

See how the moonlight
creeps along the sheets
a chalky white line
lapping down the aisle
a filmy white seam
gathering along the ward's bedposts
and out the door
caroming beyond the ward
beyond the cafeteria
beyond the clinic and the operating rooms
beyond the staff offices
past the groomed grounds
that long bendable line of moonlight
leading all the way to Dr. le Vann's office
and sitting atop the files in his cabinet.

(Le Vann, by the way, never fulfilled the administrative requirements to practice
psychiatry.)

Lacey

At night she hears beats, beats so thick
they will surely break through the tiled walls.
And if they do? Well, it's not like she can't leave the building now.
She calls her uncle every week and he sometimes takes
her to the Dairy Queen for a dipped cone.

                                               It's always quick, though.
She can't be off the grounds for long. No extended breaks.
That's what the doctor said.

A flutter in the wall. Now
she thinks something crawls behind the tiles.

She hopes something does: an animal,
a mouse, a dog, a cat, rests beside her, nuzzles
the tiles closest to her, flicks its tail in rhythm
with the thick beats, whatever they are,
wherever they come from.

Harriet

She dreams of blood, of bloody orgasms,
of swift gushes where the blood makes
a sickening pop as it passes through.

And when she wakes she finds
an entire ward of young women
staring at her. The sheets are dark,

soaked. She whimpers, lifts them, hands
shaking. She sighs. She's wet the bed.
Did you hear that, she asks them. They all nod.

Skip-rope Rhyme Outside a Calgary Apartment Building—1987

Harriet cannot have kids,
all because she was stupid!
Now she'll never find a man!
She'll live alone in cactus land!

Martin

He still smells the grass on his fingers. Even though it's been months
since they let him work outside and milk the cows and thresh
the crops. All he sees now is white, bleak and unforgiving.
He tries to align his spine with the bedsprings. They're weak
in the wrong spots. He arranges his blanket so it will cushion his back.
But then he's cold. He pulls it back over him. Kicks. Shouts.
The other boys in the ward stir but say nothing. He just did
what they themselves want to do.

A Caste System

Perry Staal, simple though he may be, recognizes
that the smarter kids get their own rooms
while he has to stay on the ward
with the dumber ones.

Before, he'd just complained because it was something to do.
Now he has a reason to complain.
But it turns out that having
a reason doesn't
help at all.

"Alberta Training School for…" That sounds a bit strange to me. Well, can mental defectives be trained. Be schooled. I don't know, it seems like a contradiction, doesn't it. I hope these people working inside—no, those—well, you can't see them now, they're not in the window anymore. But those people working inside, I hope they know what they're doing. You don't know what the hell's gonna happen around mentals. You know who's in charge here. Doctor le who. Le Vann. Never heard of him. But I bet he's got his work cut out for him. Le Vann. That sounds German. Or French, or something like that. Foreign. Actually you know, now that I think of it I have heard a bit about this place. My wife's friend's son was sent here. No, I don't know his name. Alvin, maybe. Something funny like that. Anyways, my wife told me that her friend told her that all those women, you know those loud ones from out in Ontario, McClung or something, and Murphy, the women's rights women. You know which— yeah, okay. What they did, I guess they all encouraged people to turn in their defective children. Called them the offal of society, my wife told me.

I don't know. Maybe it'd be hard. Well, what do you do if God gives you a defective child. Not like you can give it back.

Red Deer Skip-rope Rhyme

Martin, Perry, Christian, Rick,
all disgusting drooling micks!
Save us from these filthy swine!
Cage them up and feed them brine!

Court File No. 8903 20759–Edmonton; Alberta Court of Queen's Bench–January 25, 1996

"[Leilani] Muir vs. The Queen in Right of Alberta

"Action for damages in respect of wrongful sterilization and wrongful confinement.

"Summary

. . .

"The damage inflicted by the sterilization was aggravated by the associated and wrongful stigmatization of Ms. Muir as a moron, a high-grade mental defective. This stigma has humiliated Ms. Muir every day of her life, in her relations with her family and friends and with her employers and has marked her since she was admitted to the Provincial Training School for Mental Defectives on July 12, 1955, at the age of 10. Because of this humiliating categorization and treatment, the province will pay her an additional $125,000 as aggravated damages [additional to $500,280 for pain and suffering and $115,500 for interest].

. . .

"On January 18, 1959, the government sexually sterilized Ms. Muir; a bilateral salpingectomy was performed by one of a list of named surgeons; a 'routine appendectomy' was performed at the same time; Dr. le Vann assisted in the surgery. A pathology report was done on Ms. Muir's right and left Fallopian tubes. The entire length of both her Fallopian tubes were removed; the extent of the operation resulted in Ms. Muir's sterilization being irreversible. Her record contains no mention why both tubes were removed in entirety, instead of only a small section as was done in other cases. At the same time, an appendectomy was performed.

"In 1950, [Dr. le Vann] wrote an article for the *American Journal of Mental Deficiency* in which he made the following comments: 'Indeed the picture of comparison between the normal child and the idiot might almost be a comparison between two separate species. On the one hand, the graceful, intelligently curious, active young homo sapiens, and on the other the gross, retarded, animalistic, early primate type individual.'

. . .

"The circumstances of Ms. Muir's sterilization were so high-handed and so contemptuous of the statutory authority to effect sterilization, and were undertaken in an atmosphere that so little respected Ms. Muir's human dignity that the community's, and the court's sense of decency is offended...The province voluntarily gave up what would have been a complete defence to Ms. Muir's action...The effect of choosing not to use this defence is more than equivalent to an apology—it constitutes a real attempt to make things right. As a matter of policy, government apologies and initiatives of this sort to redress historical wrongs should be encouraged; punishing governments for their historical behaviour would have the opposite effect."

You Don't Feel it Until Later

One day the doctors tell Brady
that he needs to go for surgery,
an emergency
appendectomy.

He stands up. I feel fine, he says
as the orderlies roll a bed
towards him. They coax him on and he lays
back, watching the lights pass overhead.

It's a fairly standard thing,
the doctor says. *Fairly?* I don't know.
Brady looks down the hall at people watching
him as he's rolled. I don't know,

he says. Shouldn't I be feeling sick?
It's a precaution, they say. He sits up.
He hears the gurney's wheels, the clock's tick,
the nurse's light steps: *thupp thupp.*

I don't see how it's an emergency,
he says. Don't worry, they say. We'll take
good care of you. They lay him down. He just sees
a row of silver instruments lined up on a tray.

I don't need this. He rises to leave. Yes you
do. They push him back. You don't want
it to hurt, do you? No, but. Then breathe through
here. A mask over his face. A gloved hand.

Now, forty years later he tells me
how they cut open his genitals and severed
his vas deferens. It didn't hurt much then, he
says, lowering his head. I should've been more alert.

That Word

I hate that word.
What word.
Retard.
You hate it.
Yeah.
Why. You're not retarded.
I just hate it, it's an ugly word.
Okay.
How does—what does it even mean.
You don't know what it means.
Well I know what it means.
It means you're slow in the head.
I know, but I mean the word itself. Like how did it get formed.
Formed.
Yeah. Like you know how English is actually made up of a bunch of different languages.
Yeah.
Like, what word from what other language made up retard.
I don't know. German.
No.
Russian. Ukrainian. Dutch. I've heard Dutch is an ugly language.
No. Wait a minute. What if we do this. We break the word up into two, re and tard.
Okay.
Now tard is a French word, isn't it. Meaning late.
I think so.
And re means over and over again.
Right.
So, re-tard...
It means late over and over again.
Yeah. Always late.
Huh. That makes sense, I guess.
Huh.

DEAF SPEECH

I

An awkward aria
begins, blurred, bumbling,
causing crippling cacophony,
delivering discursive detritus.
Erroneous emanations echo.
Frolicking flickers forcefully
gyrate, gurgling generous
harrowing heaps, hurtling
into injurious iambs—
just junk, Joycean
kernels knotted, kiboshed.
Language loses lustre,
muscle. Methinks maybe
nobody nuzzles notions
of oscillating oratory.
Placid poetry perishes
quietly, quelling questions
regarding repressed rigour.
Simplicity seldom serves;
to think towards
undermining undulations, understand
value: vociferous vocalizations
whip without worth,
xeroxed, xenophobic, xylophagous—
yellowed, yawed yelps,
zero zestful zygotes.

What sounds do you have the most trouble with?

My Rs. Especially when I transfer from one word to the next. They sometimes sound like Ahhh rather than Rrrr.

Oh like a Brit. 'Ello bihd.

Sometimes I feel like Elmer Fudd, or like a two year old. Febwuawy. Fe-broo-awy. Awy. Ary. Gahhh.

What other sounds?

Erm, sometimes like, sometimes if I'm saying something really fast. Like Peter Piper picked a peckle. Peck of. Pickers. Peckers fuckers bastards bitches suckers of cock.

Phwoo. You know how to swear.

I know. I have no troubles there, surprisingly enough. Why do you think I swear so much? They're easy for me to say. Oh, and I hate doing the high I sounds. Like light, sight, rise. When I sing "Eye of the Tiger" I sound like I'm going through puberty. "It's the eye-EE of the tiger, it's the thrill of the fight, rising up to the challenge of our ri-EEval…" Gnaaah!

You actually sound French when you sing that.

Shut up.

Or Aussie.

That's better. I donno…you remember that book by Joyce? Portrait of the Artist? *The main character, Dedalus, he said that language is a kind of trap. I'm beginning to understand that.*

How so?

Well, like how my mouth sometimes struggles, or my tongue. Like the tail of an animal snagged in a trap, hooking, curling, swinging, lul-lul-lul-lul. Oh, and lisping. I lisp sometimes, too, don't I? Lithen to my lithping, praying Dieuf and Domb Nostrums foh thomethinks to eath. Heh.

What are you saying?

Nothing. Forget it.

elastic

I go to the bar and settle into a seat and an Australian accent which means I don't
have to settle I just speak and people believe me when I say oh yes I love Sydney,
have you ever been to the Great Barrier Reef, have you ever been to South Ad-
elaide, have you ever seen a rugby game, fuck the All-Blacks with their faggoty
Haka, no, it's okay for me to say that, you see us Aussies are more prejudiced
folk so, no, kangaroos do not roam the streets, they stay in the outback, they
only come out at night, yes, like bats, yeah I know you see them on TV and it's
daytime there, but those are just tourism advertisements meant to get you over
there, do you know that in Australia we have this ritual where if you're a boy
and you turn eighteen your friends blindfold you and take you out into the desert
and put a handful of sand on your tongue and make you sing Keith Urban songs,
yeah I had to do it, it was hard, I hate Keith Urban, he's hardly Aussie anymore.

accent

                                                                          elastic

Or I'm at the café and I order a hot chocolate (extra whipped cream) and the
woman behind the counter asks if I'm Irish, your accent reminds me of Cork,
she says, oh you don't say, I say, and she adds sprinkles to the whipped cream,
where in Ireland are you from, she says, and I accept the hot chocolate, nearly
burning my fingertips, I lean forward against the counter, do I lean into the ac-
cent, do I accentuate it, do I embellish it and tilt my mouth just so, what would
Joyce do, what would the man who wrote *A Portrait of the Artist as a Young
Man* do, he would spend ten years writing his way around the problem until
he arrived at a semblance of truth, well that's no good to me, the Irish fucker
should've gone out for hot chocolate more often, then I would decide sooner,
that what I should say is that I'm from a small town outside Dublin, in a differ-
ent county, almost its own country really, most people don't know about it, but
the people who come from this place speak in pretty much the same accent, like
the dropped E-string of a guitar, the voice slipping an octave, what's the name of
this place, she says, it doesn't have an official name, I say, but for the purposes of
this conversation we'll call it D———.

                                                                          identity

II

Acolytes act against alien alphabets,
blocking brackish bards. Blisters bubble,
chains chime, crosses crawl. Colourful
diction denotes degeneracy, discourages development.
Enraged, etymologists expel endless expletives:
fucker! Fat-ass! Fortitudinous factions form
gestures, giving ghettoized grinders galvanizing
histrionics, highlighting heresy, halting hindrances.
If I instigate impassioned inversions,
jubilantly, jocundly jouncing jawing judges,
killing killjoys, knelling Kubrickian kinetics,
lost listeners'll lull lugubrious loners.
Make minor minstrels martyrs! March
nimbly now, nudge-nudge! Nobody, no
one overrides originality. Oppressive, ossifying
practices? Piffle! Philological priests preach
quashing quirk, quadrangling quibbling quills,
racking rankling roars, ranking ragged
smart-ass schlock. Salient scops, sit
tight. The time to tear
up ultimatums *und* unleash unflinching
verbal vendettas, vaccinating venomous vagueness,
winds, waxes. We will win.
Xerography's x'd. Xenagogues x-ray xenoglossia.
Your yells'll yield yolk. Your
zealous zingers'll zing, zip, zap.

Hello, Mr. Dedalus. Welcome to D———. May I get you a coffee?

Hang on. Why are these walls so elastic? Pushpush—ah! See how they snap?

Oh, everything in D——— is like that. For the town of D———, you see, is created entirely out of language.

You toy with me. Are you serious?

Yes, Mr. Dedalus. Come with me, we'll take a walk. Oh, your coffee…mmmmmhuz-zah! Coffee! Here you are.

Astounding. A city made out of language…look! That dog is bouncing on the concrete.

That's right, Mr. Dedalus. Language is no longer a trap here. It's an elastic space, full of possibility.

And if I take these earplugs out…

Then you lose the elasticity, sir. You see Mr. Dedalus, you cannot be trapped by language if you can't hear it properly.

Well, but wouldn't you be even more trapped? Because then you'd be alone in your silence.

Being alone, Mr. Dedalus, is among the most liberating things to happen to a man. You just need to go about it properly.

Really? And how do you do that?

You make it a strategy rather than a pity.

accent

With thousands of New Zealanders I watch the All-Blacks rugby team do the
haka, a traditional dance celebrating the aboriginal Maori culture, hì, ka mate
ka mate, ka ora ka ora, aggressive stances, slap the legs, pound the chest, signs
of power, maleness, leg muscles and tattoos, the crowd singing with them, tenei
te tangata puhuruhuru, I sing with the crowd, my accent falling in, a-upane
ka-upane, a-upane ka-upane whiti te ra, hì, the players jump, the crowd jumps, I
miss the jump, I hear my own high accent, shored up against the roar.

elastic

III

Brawk-pock-pock-pock-braaaawwk-pock-pock-pock.

What's that clucking noise?

That, Mr. Dedalus, is the sound of letters fucking so they may reproduce words.

Really?

Listen. The T's getting in between the legs of the U. See? Tut-tut-tut-tut-tut.

Astounding.

Or it could just be a few chickens from that farmhouse over there. I don't know, I'm deaf!

Why don't you wear hearing aids?

Because I like my current position. It's more elastic.

Explain yourself.

If I wear hearing aids, I feel like I'm giving in, like I'm choosing a side. I'd close my-self off because I'd be submitting to a particular mode of language. I prefer to remain open, with motley linguistic strategies.

Don't you want to hear properly?

Feh. Let's talk about this later.

There is an alley in downtown D———, in the dining district, cobblestones, screen doors, garbage cans overflowing with onions and potato peelings, I like to walk down this alley during the day, even though some people find it constrictive and uncomfortable, I find it cozy, a deliciously foul wedge of space, my own little hub of the world, so one day I'm walking down the alley and I come to the point where I'm standing between the back doors of two businesses, I think they're restaurants but I can't be sure, voices spill from both sides, or at least I think they're from both sides, actually I think they're both pubs, yes Mr. Bloom we have that here for you, if you'll just have a seat, never mind Mr. Mulligan, he can be such a bitch, you'll have a Heineken will you, an Oettinger, a Guinness, a Foster's, this mosaic of accents and beer enshrouds me so that really all I have left to do is join in, and I shout fuck this American beer, drawing cheers from both sides, and I take a moment and wonder if I want to keep walking down the alley and quietly enjoy my little ovation, or go into one of the pubs and have a beer and give a face to my voice.

identity

I walk on.

What about the alphabet, then?

What about it?

Don't you find it a limiting thing? Twenty-six letters, standards of usage…

Bah! Those are merely guidelines, Mr. Dedalus. Watch this. I will magically turn an A into an O. Aaaaaaaa…O!

Okay. But those are still letters.

What about this? I shall turn your name into wine. Dedalus…mmmmmhuzzah! Wine!

Still letters. And I'm all wet now.

Christ, you're a hard man to impress, Mr. Dedalus. All right, then. What about this? (HE DELIVERS DOLLOPS OF INCOMPREHENSIBLE GIBBERISH.)

.

..

…

..

.

Wow. That's quite a lot of gibberish.

Thank you. Indeed it is, Mr. Dedalus.

But it's meaningless now.

Whaaa! The hell with you! Gibberish has its place, Mr. Dedalus.

I'm not so sure.

You only think it has no meaning because you think language must have form to be meaningful. It makes you laugh, doesn't it? You laughed.

Yes.

And is laughter not meaningful? What is the purpose of language if not to get each other laughing?

Dance of Tongues

Let us project ourselves upon the fray
(Anow-ow Anow-ow)
The silent storm is about to break
(Ka-kraaaaaaaa Ka-kraaaaaaaa)
The silent storm waxes fiercer
(Yoom-hiii Yoom-hiii)
Let us lift each other up
On a wave of voice
Tongues dancing, come what may
Let the storm be unleashed
Rawrrrrsssshk Rawrrrrsssshk our
woa-woa-woa-woa-woa tongues
krk-krk-ki-ki-krk-krk-ki-ki-krk-krk-ki-ki-krk-krk dance
shp-shp-shp-shp-shp-shp-shp to
yurrrrrrrrrrrrrrm yeh yurrrrrrrrrrrrrrrrrrrrm yeh yurrrrrrrrrrrrrrrrrrrm their
yikkity yokkity yarkity yap yikkity yokkity yarkity yap yikkity yokkity yarkity yap own
pluh-plah pluh-plah-plah pluh-plah pluh-plah-plah melody
brrrr-bikka-bikka-brrr-bikka-bikka-brrr-bikka-bikka-brr-ah!

I construct my own alphabet, a deaf speech, a dithyrambunctious voice, displacing assonance and harmony, jingleefully rutrooting in the soppingwet detritus of my verbal effluvium.

My speech is my künstlerroman,
punctuated by s
        lips of the tongue.

Ass,
bitch, bastard, balls,
cunt, cocksucker,
dick, dork, dong,
fuck, fart,
prick, pecker, piss, pussy,
hell,
goddamn,
jackoff,
muff,
tit, twat,
shit…

whatever.

Now I know my ABCs, won't you come and sing with me?

BEAUTIFUL MUTANTS

CHANCE

Shot

It's getting harder to find a vein.

Chance pats the pocked crook of his elbow, the skin ruined, like the scarred remains of chicken pox scratches. His buddy told him yesterday his boss had to dig a hole for a sewage pipe. They tried three times and then had to move to another site because the soil was too unstable and had been dug up too much already.

Chance lays the syringe on the table and slides his seat back and props his foot on the table's edge. He takes off his sock and taps his foot to coax up the vein and takes the syringe and pushes it into the vein and holds up his foot so it drains up to his head. The air thickens as he sighs, dozes.

A cold breeze and the smell of McDonald's wake him. His leg is still up on the table and it creaks as he lowers it. Teresa puts the bag of food on the table, the paper soaked through with grease.

"Another one already?" she says, taking off her coat and nodding at the syringe.

Chance opens the bag and pulls out a quarter pounder with cheese and begins eating.

Teresa picks up the syringe.

"Second one today?"

"Third," through a mouthful of burger.

"It's only one in the afternoon."

"So?"

"You save any for me?"

"I'll get more later."

"With what? You have no money."

"Craig'll give me some."

"Craig?"

"Jackson's brother."

"Isn't he a criminal?"

"Eh, sorta kinda."

Teresa sits down. "How'd you pay for this one if you have no money?"

"I promised him money."

"You promised who money?"

"The guy."

"What guy?"

"The guy I got the needles from."

"You don't know his name?"

"No. But he knows my name, so it's okay."

"You promised money to a dealer you don't know?" Teresa takes the fries from the bag. "And are you allowed to go to Craig?"

"Why not?"

"Isn't that like a no-no, changing dealers?"

"Craig's not a dealer, he's a friend."

"What if that guy finds out?"

"Don't worry about it."

Chance wipes his fingers on the bag and takes the fries from Teresa, who takes a chicken sandwich out of the bag.

"Don't do anything stupid," she says.

"Yeah," through a mouthful of fries.

He feels pleasurably lazy, like he's been permitted to be idle. He stares towards the living room at the Scarface rug on the wall, at the sword he made in metal-work three years ago. On the coffee table in front of the couch a smattering of pipes and roaches remain. He wonders if the roaches will be enough for the evening.

"When will you go?" Teresa says.

"Go?"

"To see Craig."

"I don't know. Probably go later."

"I have to work tonight."

"Okay."

"So please get it before I go. I work at seven."

"Do you get paid tonight?"

"No. Not until Friday."

Chance glances around. "What day is it today?"

"Tuesday."

"When's the rent due?"

"Friday."

"Okay."

"When's your EI run out?"

"I don't know. I think it's gone soon."

"You need to get a job," she says.

"I know," he says.

"Seriously, Chance."

"I know."

"Could you go see Craig?"

"Right now?"

"If not now, then soon."

"Wait till I'm finished eating."

"Fine."

Chance smiles, his cheeks puffed out with a mouthful of fries.

*

Craig lives on Pine in downtown Prince George, a few blocks from the McDonald's on Victoria. A musk of dirt and cigarettes curls up from under the door. Chance knocks five times and no one answers. He tries to look in the window but the curtains obscure the view and all he can see is a section of carpet and a few magazines. He goes to George Street and finds no one but poor people. On Third Avenue he sees someone familiar and asks where he can get some scag and is pointed to a house just off of Tabor. He knocks on the door.

The guy who gave him the needles answers.

"Oh, hey, it's you," the guy says. "Come in."

Chance steps inside. The carpet's thick under his shoes. A trace of Glade hangs in the air. The guy walks with a waddle, his wide, soggy belly stretching out the hem of his red hoodie.

"What's going on?" Chance says.

"Just taking it easy. I've got *This is Spinal Tap* on downstairs. You ever see it?"

"Think I've seen a little bit of it."

"Good fucking movie, man," the guy says. "Great fucking movie." He opens his arms. "So! Do you come bearing good tidings?"

"What?"

"Did you bring me some money?"

"Oh." Chance steps back and wipes his shoes on the threshold. "Actually, if it's all right, I need some more horse, and a few needles."

"You need needles? What was wrong with the last ones I gave you?"

"Nothing's wrong with them. I used them."

"You can't use them again? Those things are expensive."

"I know." Chance shrugs. "Maybe I can use them again."

"Yeah." The guy sits on a chair in the living room. "So, you don't have any money?"

"Not this time, but I will on Friday."

The guy adjusts himself in his seat, plopping his hands on the armrests. He studies Chance for a minute, then sniffles and wipes his nose.

"I don't know why I'm sitting down, I'm missing my movie. Come downstairs with me."

"Okay."

"We'll get you some horse."

"And some syringes?"

"And some syringes."

The guy takes his time in getting up from his chair. He stretches his back when he stands.

When Chance emerges from the house twenty minutes later, his pockets stuffed with syringes and heroin, he walks down the street and into the alley. He tucks himself behind a garage and removes the syringes and begins to count them.

"Hey."

Chance looks up and sees a man wearing a Prince George Cougars jacket.

Chance stuffs the syringes back into his pocket. The man looks like an ex–hockey player: at least six-foot-three, heavy in the shoulders and with a round but solid gut. His hair is black and shaved almost to the scalp.

"What're you doing, man?" Chance says.

"Were you just in there with Alphonse?" the man says.

"Alphonse? Who's Alphonse?"

"The guy in that house."

Chance turns his head. "Oh, is his name Alphonse? Heh heh, Alphonse…"

"Yeah, man." The man points at Chance's pockets. "What'd he give you?"

Chance fixes his hands in his pockets. "Give me? He didn't give me anything."

"What'd I see in your pockets there?"

"I don't have anything in my pockets."

"You have horse in there? How much did it cost you?"

"It's not your business, man."

"Here, man, I'll buy it from you, okay?"

Chance scoffs. "What? The hell with you. Go get your own."

"C'mon, just let me have one syringe, one packet."

"Fucks to you, man. These are mine."

"C'mon, man. Just one."

"This is my fuckin stuff. Go get your own."

"Alphonse won't sell to me anymore."

"Well, too fuckin bad. That's not my fault, man."

The man extends his open palm. "Give one to me," he says. "Just one."

Chance starts to walk past the man. He shoves Chance against the garage and tries for Chance's pockets. Chance whips his bony fists upwards, smacks the man in the chin. He kicks him in the shins, drives his knuckle into his eye. The man cringes; he grabs Chance by the jacket and pulls him into his punch. The blow splashes in Chance's stomach; Chance buckles. The man's fingers root in his pockets. He snaps his leg up and boots the man in the testicles. The man seizes.

"Ah! You...fucking faggot!"

Chance starts to run. The man, still holding Chance by the jacket, gives a swift jerk and yanks him to the ground. Chance lands face-first.

"Hey!"

The man lands on his back, his knee digging. He grabs Chance by the hair and shoves his head into the gravel. In Chance's eyes the ground whorls, coils. The colours of individual pebbles surprise him. Words arise in spurts: "Piece of...faggot..." The two roll and scuffle. Despite his thin frame Chance is able to thrust his thumb into the man's eye. The man cries out as Chance finds grip on his temple and squeezes.

"Stop! Faggot!"

Using his long reach the man holds Chance back by his chin. Chance doesn't see the pistol until two shots go off; he hears the shots after the fact. Then the black handgun glints, the pale sunshine sliding along its narrow grooves. He lies there, stunned. He and the man meet eyes. The man pants, looks surprised. They watch each other for a moment. A strange sensation arises from Chance's belly, like hot water is repeatedly dropping on the same spot. Ache slowly shifts from his face to his gut. The man shakes his head and goes through Chance's pockets with ease. Then he runs.

Chance remains on the ground, wondering why the sky is so grey.

BEAUTIFUL MUTANTS

I

Sandra can't put her lipstick on herself since she turned blind and bought into Saramago's phrase that to be dead is to be blind. So she imagines herself as a cadaver, lips, skin and hair drained of colour, lying spread-eagled and still.

The trouble is she feels things differently. Different spaces have opened in her: yawning ventricles, dark and resonant. She hunches and squeezes against them but it's like trying to will shut the walls of her heart. She tries to convince herself she is less worthy of feeling, that wind blows around her as though around a post. She knows people talk behind her back. Her blindness softens her, so people either aren't as afraid of being direct or are even more reserved. As though everything is about her eyes. She swings her cane and puts a hole in the wall, glad of the loud thud and the crinkling drywall as she pulls it out.

*

In the morning Lily slips out of her wheelchair and onto a long plastic sled, already loaded with seeds, fertilizer, plant food and tools. Before she pushes herself along the ground, she unrolls the hose and hooks its spray nozzle to the sled's pullstring. Then she goes to the garden.

The rows are thin to allow her space to push herself between them. She can only grow so many things. Carrots. Peas. Things that need only a little room. Reaching from the sled she digs and overturns the earth, inserts the seeds and covers them. And just as she turns the hose on the rows it begins to rain.

*

Jared sits in the back seat watching his schoolmates. As he swings his gaze he catches his reflection in the window. His lips seem crooked, pushed out of place. His schoolmates dart past outside, disrupting his reflection like sparrows disrupting fog. One girl sees him and averts her eyes; the familiar chill of inciting discomfort flares through his shoulders. He reacts. He doesn't want to but he's just geared that way. He swats the window. Elbows banging. Funny bone alarm. He shouts.

Jared calm down. His mother starts the car and drives off, thinking someone outside said something. His reflection shifts again and again he reacts.

II

Sandra. What. What're you doing. Nothing. Put that away. No. Put it down. No. Stop, give it to me. Sandra.

Her husband takes a golf club from her and throws it into the corner. Seizes her. Wrestles her. She punches him. Sobs.

What the hell were you doing. I hate this. Hate what. Blindness. Well why the hell'd you have my golf club. I needed to hit something. Sandra just because you're angry. No not because I'm angry. Then why. Because I needed to feel free. I needed to have some time where I didn't have to worry about walking into a table or a chair. I wanted to expand, create my own space, rule over my own space. And not have the space rule me.

Her husband wipes her eyes and tells her he's looking into them. This is their habit now. He tells her when their eyes meet. So they can maintain.

Can you understand that. Yes.

*

The night before, Lily had dreamt of plants sprouting from rock: orchids with tissue-paper petals stretching out of boulders, conical clusters of purple lilacs punching through volcanic rock, their scent softening the bitter air.

The rain splashes in the dirt which soon becomes mud. Lily's sled soon fills up and she starts to push herself out of the garden, her hands sinking into the mud. She doesn't travel more than two feet before she runs into a deep thick puddle and becomes stuck.

She slides to the bottom of the sled so her legs come up against the lip. She pushes and starts to rock, but the mud spills into the sled, and the rain is cold on her face and shoulders, and the more she pushes the deeper the sled sinks. She rocks harder and the sled lodges in and the mud sloshes around her, and she shoves her legs against the lip one last time and then sits hunched over and panting.

*

The mechanical makeup of his body tilts. Jared's head tilts. Like he's always wondering or trying to see underneath.

He knows what he has. Most people think he doesn't know but he knows. He braces against them.

When he talks his words are not his own. Palsy's. Like a friend. Invisible. Hey Palsy what's happening.

Jared. Yeuh. Can you come set the table please. Sits Marger's sturn. No she did it last night. Neeoh. Jared don't make excuses, just set the table. Be careful with the knives. Mmnoh.

III

Sandra's husband comes home one day and finds her in the kitchen stirring sugar into a cup of tea, her cane folded up on the island counter. He turns off the burner and takes her hand. She reaches out and lowers her free hand onto his shoulder, having long since memorized his dimensions. In her hand he puts a small folder. She holds it for a moment and opens it and rubs the long waxen card, runs her finger along its printer-serrated edge.

What. We leave in five days. Where. You always wanted to go. What. You're serious. Yes. Rome. Italy. Yes. No. Yes. No. Yes we're going. Why what's the point now. Why not. I can't see what I wanna see, what I wanted to see. You can still say you went there. It won't mean anything. How do you know.

*

The rain performs a thrumming march on the plastic sled. Lily's tools and bags of seed are overtaken by mud. The remaining holes she dug for the seeds are filled with rain. She puts her palms down on the sled and over the course of a few minutes feels the mud level slowly rise up to her wrists. The mud inches up and over her legs, her hips. She closes her eyes and holds her hands up to the rain, the drops splashing on her eyelids, her fingers branching out, the mud cool around her trunk.

*

In his bedroom Jared has a poster of Georges St-Pierre. St-Pierre crouches in fighting stance. Eyes narrowed. Stalking. Jared stands in front of it. He doesn't much care about how St-Pierre looks or how intimidating he is. He cares about the way his arms look. How the elbows are bent like his own. The knobs the same. Always fighting. When he makes fists red strength wells up. Wants to hit something. Did once. Was grounded. Dad had a black eye for a month.

IV

A week later Sandra and her husband stand in line at the Vatican Museum, walking through the metal detectors at the security station. Sandra's stopped briefly so her cane can be inspected, and then the two of them walk down the vaulted corridors. He describes the lavish carpets and tapestries draped over the walls, identifies the busts and statues, the voices of all the other people hushed and polite. She wishes she could touch the statues, feel the contours and ridges of the marble. White signs direct everyone towards la Cappella Sistina. No cameras. No video recorders.

The halls wind up and down, swathed in holy, philosophical and military art. Sandra and her husband round a short corner, the nub of her cane stubbing against the wall, and he says Ah, a few steps up, four, and the voices instantly slip to whispers.

A smell like sweetened dust. Footsteps ring up from the marble floor and Sandra senses that the space around her has opened, that the ceiling has risen. She inhales, keeping her breathing quiet. Her husband guides her to the middle of the chapel so that she stands underneath the portrait of God reaching out to give Adam life. She stills herself, standing slightly apart from her husband, giving him her cane. She keeps her gaze forward, raising her arms, holding open her hands, letting the mysticism provoke her, like how Adam, with his finger bent and his body relaxed, lets God animate him. Her skin feels thickened. A warm, rousing presence enshrouds her, as though her skin glows. Her breathing deepens and her face goes hot. She tenses her muscles and locks her joints, alarmed at the effervescence she feels. People whisper to each other and their shoulders brush her hands but she remains rooted, her heart full and stirring. It's beautiful, her husband says. I know, she says.

*

Lily sighs, arches her back. The rain slips down her throat. Tastes like lake water. She rolls out of the sled and into the dirt and mud. Clumps stick to her arms; she shakes them off. Aware of how ridiculous she looks. How fascinating. How beautiful. She stays outside awhile longer before boosting herself along the ground and going inside, laughing as she drags mud all over the linoleum and hardwood.

*

Jared sits at the kitchen table drinking milk, enjoying the quiet. The house seems to yawn and decompress around him. He enjoys the blankness of the kitchen wall, the soft degrees of sunlight as it stretches across the linoleum, the table's oaken slickness accentuated by the absence of placemats and vases.

After each sip he rolls the milk within his glass. The milk, cool and rich, lingers wherever it's tipped, consistently leaving behind its traces and whitening the insides of the dense blue glass. When Jared sets the glass down its walls are coated with undulating white curves that fade slightly and then remain.

With a clatter of car keys and heeled pumps his mother enters carrying a box with a green towel draped over it. Jared sighs. Brings his glass closer. Finishes the milk.

Hi Jared. Hey. Have you eaten. Nnno. Were there any phone calls. No.

She sets the box on the counter, takes off her shoes, then puts the box on the table in front of him. She pulls up a chair. Jared studies the box; its sharp dimensions suggest solidity.

Jared. Yeah. While I was on my way downtown I was doing some thinking, and I know that things have been difficult for you. Sometimes school is tough, sometimes it's not what you want it to be, sometimes you and I get angry at each other. It happens. Yeauh. You grrrrind your way throoough it. That's right. That's how life is.

His mother puts her hand atop the box.

Whut iss that. I know I don't show it and that I often kick you in the ass, but I'm very proud of you, Jared. I think that with school and everything, you've handled yourself admirably. In fact, you're more mature than most teenagers I've seen. Whut. Yeah, it's true. You're much more sympathetic towards other people. Zymmmpathetig how. You're actually able to feel and understand another person's pain, or joy. You're much more genuine. Oh.

His mother lifts a corner of the towel, revealing a glass tank. Jared leans in.

I stopped at the pet store on the way home. Whut is it.

She removes the towel. A desert landscape has been taped to the tank's back wall. The floor is carpeted with sand and black and green pebbles. A plastic water dish sits in the corner. From underneath a rock curls the glinting black tail of a scorpion.

Jared's mouth opens, his eyes glossy with fascination. He looks at his mother.

Fer me. Yes. Heezmine. She is yours, yes. You can put her in your room, but you have to be careful when you take her out of the tank, okay.

Jared chuckles. Laughs. He and his mother meet eyes and smile at one another.

CHANCE

Recovery

Chance rouses full of that lazy feeling. When he realizes he's in bed, he goes back to sleep.

He wakes again stiff with pain. He can't flex his legs or his back. The room is dark and smells of stale food and bleached laundry. The bed has a thick plastic rail along the sides and at the end and a thin tube leads into his arm.

"Hey."

He sits up and it's difficult because his legs don't counterbalance. Sensation has been emptied from them. He groans and leans forward and pokes them with both hands.

"Hey."

He starts at the knees and feels nothing. He works his way up his thighs, hands jittery, prodding and pinching the skin, moving back and forth from one leg to the other; reaching between his legs he grabs his testicles and hisses at the pain he feels there.

A nurse enters the room and flips on the light. Chance winces.

"Hey!"

"Oh, you're up." She approaches the bed. "How do you feel?"

"Why can't I feel my legs?"

"Do you feel nauseous?"

"No. Why can't I feel my legs?"

"One of the bullets—you remember being shot?"

Chance rolls his eyes. "Yes."

"One of the bullets entered your spine. We took the other one out of your intestine."

"It hit my spine?"

"Yes."

Chance groans. Shuts his eyes. "So…it went, like, deep? As in it's serious?"

The nurse bites her lip. "Yeah."

"So you're saying…"

"Yes."

He sighs. Scrunches the blanket in his hands. "And…and this is permanent?"

The nurse nods. Chance takes a moment, stares at his legs. His face blanches.

"Do you want me to call your girlfriend? She was here earlier."

Chance doesn't answer. The nurse leaves the room. When the door closes Chance punches the bed, the railings. He hits his legs by accident. Then on purpose. Screams.

When Teresa arrives she enters the room crying. She hugs Chance and he hugs her back and cries too. They fold into one another and remain that way for a long time.

Then Teresa sits on the bed beside him and holds his hand and squeezes it, and although it hurts, Chance doesn't say so. He lets his head sink back into the pillow, and swallows and the saliva isn't enough to lubricate his voice, so he drinks from the cup of day-old water on the tray beside the bed.

"The police wanna talk to you," Teresa says.

"Okay."

"Do you know who did it?"

"I don't know the guy, but I remember what he looks like. Tall, solid son of a bitch. Had a Cougars jacket on."

"Cougars? You mean like the hockey team?"

"Yeah."

"Was he a teenager or an older guy?"

"Think he was in his thirties or forties. Big fucking guy."

"I heard a lot of kids from the rep teams take drugs."

"Probably they do. Even the coaches fucking do it, I bet."

"Yeah." Teresa shakes her head. "Maybe it was a coach you saw."

"Maybe. Probably." Chance shrugs. "Why the hell would a coach be involved with drugs?"

"Why would a coach have a handgun?"

"Yeah. Good question."

"'Cause they're supposed to be coaching, right? Setting an example and all that."

"That's right. I want an answer to that question."

Teresa squeezes his hand again. Digs her nails into it. Chance grunts.

"Well, fuck," he says. "What do we do now?"

"I don't know." Teresa sighs. "You'll come home, I guess. We'll get you into a wheelchair. We'll take things from there."

Chance groans. "Wheelchair."

"What else can you do, Chance? You can't walk or anything."

"I'll be in a fucking wheelchair. Like those poor fucking natives down on George Street. You know who I'm talking about? I'll be watching people pass me, I'll be looking up at people all the time."

"Yeah. Well, you're short, so you do that anyway."

"Shut up."

Teresa chuckles. "It'll take some time. We'll have to make some adjustments. We'll have to clean all your clothes out of the hallway so you have room to move."

"*My* clothes? Your fuckin bras are always hanging off the goddamn doorknob!"

"That's because they're drying. We don't have a laundry rack."

"Whatever." Chance bucks, jerks his blanket up when his legs don't follow. "How the fuck am I gonna get around?"

"In a wheelchair."

"What about in the winter?" Chance says. "I'll get snow all over the wheels and it'll get all thick and shit, and then I can't move."

"I'll put non-stick cooking spray on the wheels so you don't have to worry about it."

Chance groans. "And what about driving?"

"What about driving? You don't drive."

"No, but I wanted to. I was gonna learn how to drive."

"Well, you still can."

"Christ. I'd need one of those special cars, like the ones on the show with the midget people where everything's done by hand."

"Yeah, that'd be fitting for you, seeing how short you are."

"You're shorter than me, you frickin wench."

"But I'm a girl. It's okay for me to be short."

Chance smiles a little. Pats his knees. He rubs his thigh muscles tenderly. He looks at them as though they're generous cheques he can't cash.

"Are you gonna be all right?" Teresa says.

Chance sniffles. "It's all bullshit," he says. "Even if the guy is caught..." He gestures at his legs. "Fuck!"

Teresa puts her hand on his shoulder. "You know, I've stopped using," she says.

Chance looks up at her. "Oh yeah?"

"After this happened, it didn't seem right. It seems pointless. You know what I mean?"

"Yeah."

"Are you gonna stop using?"

"Probably. I've been hooked up to this shit, so I'm good." Chance nods up at the IV. "And I'm not crazy about being shot again."

"That's probably why you're not going through withdrawal. They asked me when they brought you in if you took drugs. I told them yeah."

"Yeah."

"When you get out of here we'll have to get you a job."

Chance raises his eyebrows. "A job?"

"Yeah."

"Can I even work?"

"Well, yeah. Why not?"

Chance makes a face and nods at his legs.

"So what? You have your arms, you have your head."

"This is fucking Prince George. It's nothing but mill jobs and shit." Chance lifts his arms and flexes. "And I'm no Brock Lesnar or Einstein or whatever."

"Maybe you can build up your arms or something. Rick Hansen did it."

"Who the hell is Rick Hansen?"

"You know, the guy who—"

"Oh yeah, the wheelchair guy. Meh, I don't know. I don't think I'm as good as that."

"What do you mean you're not as good?"

"I mean I'm not that kind of person."

"What kind of person?"

"The hardworking kind."

Teresa raises her eyebrows. "Well Chance, I think you have to become hardworking. I know it'll be hard and I know you'll bitch and complain, but you better fucking become hardworking, 'cause I'm not pushing your ass all over the place when you get out of here."

"What the hell, Teresa? Take it easy on me, eh?"

"You know that your EI's gonna run out?"

"Who cares about fucking EI right now?"

"I'm the one who has to take care of everything while you're in here. I'm gonna try and find you a decent wheelchair, and then when you come home next month—"

"Next month?"

"—or in a few weeks, whenever it is, you can start looking for jobs."

"Teresa, don't you think you're moving a bit fast here?"

"Things have to change, Chance. Things *have* changed. You gotta make a move."

Chance sighs. Teresa continues to talk and he tunes out. He turns towards the window, peering at the hospital courtyard through a wedge between the curtains. It's May. Late snow has left the grass a deep brown. Green is only hinted at. Beside the gazebo an elderly woman sits in her wheelchair, alone, feeding the birds. Sparrows hop around and peck the ground at her feet. Chance watches her for a long time, confused about why the woman seems so peaceful.

ASYMMETRY

Every night it's the same: before going to bed,
Zach studies himself in the mirror.
He cups what remains of his leg, pleased
with the patchy hairlessness where it has been cut off;
the stub's smooth curve, the way his boxer briefs neatly
augment it, the contour of shadow
on the boxer leg, sewed shut.

Since he turned fourteen he's embraced
the blank space, the airy hollow of his jeans before
he ties them off, the lightness he feels
when he swings himself forward on his crutches,
his body a pendulum. The medical term
for his above-the-knee cut has assumed its own music:
transfemoral amputation, a response to peripheral necrosis
caused by sepsis. The words roll off his tongue
whenever someone asks. Especially girls.

Leaning on the wall, he locks his bedroom door
and goes to the desk and cocks the lamp, angling it into the corner
so he'll appear darker. Then he repositions himself before
the mirror and watches himself pull off his briefs. He exhales
at the stub, softened by the dim light. He turns his body slightly—
his cock flares. He loves how the stub
makes it look bigger. He leans on the wall and flexes
his biceps, pleased with his upper body's symmetry
and the disproportion between arms and legs.

He squeezes his sharp hipbones and traces the swales
where his abdominals segue into his waist,
his crotch. He's glad he's skinny. He makes amputation look
almost fashionable. He angles up his head and pushes out

his chest. He holds the pose for as long as he can,
stilling his breath, keeping his eyes open and fixed
in a seductive stare. When he finally takes a breath he puts
his hand on the wall and ambles over
to his computer and turns it on.
Then he takes his camera and stands in front
of the mirror again, resuming his statuesque pose.

Zach. What. Are you going to bed. Yeah in just a minute. Are you reading.
Yeah. Okay. I saw the light on, I was just gonna go downstairs and make some
Triscuits and ham if you want some. No thanks Mom. Okay. Have a good sleep.
Goodnight. Goodnight.

He waits for a moment before turning on
the camera and setting the timer.

*

In the morning he watches where he puts his crutches
to ensure they don't mark the hardwood floor,
watches for a glint of water or milk on the kitchen tiles.
One time the rubber stub of his crutch
landed on a spill and he slipped and dislocated his arm.
Afterwards there was such a commotion
about school that eventually his parents decided to keep him at home
for two weeks. He loved it, settling on the couch
and watching *Friday the 13th* movies.

His mother watches him enter. Has his lunch
prepared for him on the counter. He sits at the table
and props his crutches against the wall and reaches for the box
of Lucky Charms. His mother joins him.

Did you sleep well. Yeah, all right. That's good. Mom, I have a question. Yeah.
Can we put some carpet down in the living room. I don't wanna slip again

and it's just a pain in the ass to be careful all the time. Well we can look at that, though it might take a while. Okay. Of course, if you got a prosthetic like your dad and I keep saying, you wouldn't have to be careful all the time. I don't want a prosthetic, Mom. Why not. I said before, 'cause they're geeky and they look uncomfortable. You haven't even tried one on, and nobody would even notice because it's all under your jeans. I would notice. I don't want a wooden leg or plastic leg clicking along while I'm walking. I'd feel like the goddamn Terminator. But it'd help you. I prefer being this way. Why. I just do. Okay.

His mother sighs and takes a handful
of Lucky Charms from the box. Zach takes too big a spoonful
and some of the milk dribbles onto his chin.
On the way to school he tells himself to check
his favourite website to see how many
of its chat members use prosthetics.

*

In the first year he was sexually active a small wart appeared
at the top of his prick. At first he was angry, calling the girl he'd fucked last
to tell her she was a whore
and that her cunt was a den for creepy crawlies.
But when he decided to have it checked out at the sex clinic, something changed.
He thought of how he'd be seen: a fifteen year old amputee
swinging his way into the clinic with a toothy grin and red cheeks.
The other patients in the waiting room watched him
as he told the receptionist his name. One of the girls looked at him
as though to say Seriously. One of the guys, an older man
who looked like he'd spent his life watching Grateful Dead concert footage,
made a face as though to say Awesome or Way to go, man.
Zach had worn the boxers with the ants and beetles on them, just to see
how the doctor would react. When she said nothing
he asked her how she liked his boxers and she said
The message carries through. He smiled and she smiled back, folding back
his prick to ensure the wart was alone.

When he left with a prescription in his pocket
he briefly thought about collecting STIs the same way others collect crystals,
letting them crowd his cock until it looked
like mould growing. But no. One was enough.

*

Later that night he logs on to "Off Balance," a website
for amputee swingers on which he's posted pictures of himself.
As he checks his email a melody of fetishes arises:
acrotomophilia, apotemnophilia—those who fuck amputees
and those who want to be fucked as amputees.
Last week he was online and chatted with a woman
who'd had her hand cut off by a lawnmower
and declared she'd never use a vibrator again.

I like the feel of a fistless arm. Really. Doesn't that feel weird. No, I really love it.
It doesn't hurt or anything. 'Cause it's all bony and shit, it's not soft like a dick.
Well I've been around a bit sweetie, so it doesn't hurt one bit. It's actually really
wonderful. Do you have anything taken off. My leg. What happened. Peripheral
necrosis caused by sepsis. I see. It means rot. I know what it means. Where do
you live. Do you use a prosthetic.

He never tells them where he lives. He's smarter than that.
He has met a few women through the site—in public,
well-lit places. They turned out all right. One had had both
her arms removed while she was still in the womb,
so she was very much in touch with her legs and her abdomen.
The strange strengths of these women never cease to impress him.
They never ask him his age—his profile says he's twenty, and with
the right clothes he looks the part. He never fucks women over thirty.
It's not right. His favourite is Katana, who is pale and tattooed.
They see each other every few weeks. She's twenty-five and shy
with a below-the-knee lop—transtibial. They bug each other over whose term
sounds better and who's had more flesh removed. He wins

in amputation terms, but she has tattoos all over her body
so pain works in her favour. She uses a prosthetic for everything
except sex, because, in her words, It fucks with your alignment.

They lay there, spent. The lights of a passing car squeeze through
the curtains on her bedroom window. Zach shifts
onto his full leg side, facing her.

You don't think it's a compromise, he says. What do you mean, she says. Your
prosthetic. What about it. You don't think it's a cop-out, or a mask, you know,
disguising what you really are. That's only part of who I am. It doesn't feel odd
to you. Not really. Why, are you thinking about getting one. No, I don't think
I can. Why not. I know this may sound stupid, Zach says, but it'd feel like I
was conforming. I like being different. We're all different. Look at me. Yeah,
but. But—just wanting to be different is no excuse for making things harder
for yourself. And you're still different, you're still missing a leg. You still get to
weird people out, except this time it's more subtle. You understand. Yeah.

Katana pokes him on the nose and asks him his real age.
Zach says eighteen. She gives a look like she knows he's lying
but she says nothing. They both know they're lucky to have each other
for the moment. Zach says he will tell her his real age
when he's old enough. She chuckles and shakes her head.

You wanna see me again, she says. Yes. Pretty soon we're gonna have to make
this official, she says. Maybe, he says. How do you feel about that. I could go for
it. Have you ever dated anyone exclusively. A few girls, not very many. How
long did they last. A few weeks each, maybe a month. Why so quickly. They
bored me. I see. And do I bore you. No. Hell no.

She drives Zach to the edge
of his street and they kiss and he meanders lazily
down the road, enjoying how the streetlights lend
the overcast their glow. When he gets home he enters through
the kitchen. His mother's sitting at the table
reading a War Amps pamphlet.

Hey Zach, she says. Were you out again. Yeah, he says. Out with a friend. Which friend. A girl friend. You have a girlfriend. No. Well, sorta. That's wonderful, Zach. Why didn't you tell us. I don't know. What's her name. Katana. Katana. That's an unusual name. I like it. She go to your school. No. What school does she go to. I don't think she goes to school. What do you mean. How'd you meet her. Online. You met her online. Yeah. You met her through a website. Yeah. Zach. What. Which website is it. Just this one website, what's the deal. Zach, your father and I told you before, we don't want you going on those websites. I know. You never know what kind of people you're getting involved with. I don't want some thirty-year-old nutcase calling our house again, asking after you. This is different, though. How is it different. Well, I've reached the age of consent, right. The age of consent. Yeah, I've reached the right age. The right age. Just how old is your girlfriend. Just a little older than me. How much older. A year, give or take a few years. Show me this website. I wanna see it.

His mother stands, leaving the pamphlet on the table.
Zach rises. His crutch slips from his chair and clatters on the floor.

No no no, Mom, you don't have to see it. Why not. Because. You might find it weird. What do you mean weird. You might find it offensive. Offensive. Erhm… The fact that I'd find it offensive is a bit alarming, Zach. Uhm. Let's go upstairs to your room and you can show me the website. I don't want to. Then you can show me on my computer down here. No. Why. What exactly is on this website, Zach. Are there questionable people on there. Ah, depends what you mean by questionable. Are there people on this site that you wouldn't invite into our home. I guess you could say that. Are there naked people on this website. Naked people. Don't lie to me, Zach.

Zach sighs and lets his mother lead him down the hall.
Forty-five minutes later, his "Off Balance" profile deleted and his ears swollen with his mother's shrieks, he calls Katana
to ask if they can make it official.

*

High school bored him anyway.
He finds a job as the inventory guy at an auto parts store
and continues his schoolwork through correspondence.
He and Katana rent an apartment downtown
just beside a bus stop, across from the native arts centre. Zach doesn't care
where it is as long as it has carpets and wide hallways.

The apartment's colour scheme soon exhausts him. The red
and black 1970s carpet seems to loom upwards and rise as he swings
down the hall. The dimpled walls give him headaches.
The whole building smells of paint and stale fabric.
It doesn't help that Katana owns a lamp
with an orange shade draped over top. The light settles heavily upon
the living room, spread-eagled on the walls, licking
the shaded corners. One night they have sex
on the couch and Zach's head swoons as though he's tripping
and Katana has to get off him so he can hang his head between
his knee and his stub and reclaim his bearings.

The next night he and Katana attend a punk rock show. Katana leaves him
standing along the wall while she jostles her way to the stage.
She leans forward and bangs her head
and screams back at the vocalist. Zach finds a chair and sits down,
annoyed, his ears hot with pounding bass.
When the band finishes its set Katana stumbles on her way
back to him. She falls on the gymnasium floor and Shit!
and grabs her leg at the point where the prosthetic meets the stub.
Zach starts towards her but someone else helps her up
and to the bathroom. Twenty minutes later she emerges with an even more
pronounced limp. She leans on Zach and he almost loses
his balance. She smells like pot.

Let's go outside. What. It's too hot in here. What. It's too loud in here. Zach I
can't hear you, let's go outside.

Everyone is outside. Most of them drink or smoke. It's dark.
Silver beer cans skid across the grass. A guy with a face
painted like the Crow lights up a purple pipe.
Zach glances around. Katana asks him if he wants a drink. He says no.

What are you thinking, she says. Nothing, he says. Are you okay. Yeah. Are
you uncomfortable. Yeah. Why. This isn't my crowd. I thought you liked punk.
I do but I'm too—this isn't my crowd. You're too young. No. Yeah. You're
under eighteen aren't you. No I'm not, not anymore. But before you moved in. I
turned eighteen last month. Are you lying. No.

Katana pulls her hair back from her face.
The fairy tattoo on her arm seems to glow;
its outline glimmers under the streetlights. She asks Zach if
he wants to go home. He says that she can stay and he'll take
the bus. We'll talk later, Katana says. Okay. He plants
his crutches and swings himself up the street,
balancing himself long enough to boot an empty beer can down the sidewalk.

*

Have you talked to your parents lately, Katana says. Not since I left. Why not.
'Cause I don't want to, Zach says. Do you think they miss you. I bet they miss
you. They said they didn't want me in their house. They were angry with you,
they'd just found out their son was a perv. I'm not a perv. Yeah you are. No I'm
not. What's the big deal. I'm a perv, too. It's not about being a pervert, though,
he says. It's about, like, finding people like me and being around people like
me. It was like they couldn't understand that, he says, or they couldn't accept it.
That's why they kept asking me to get a prosthetic. Okay, Katana says, but you
didn't have to put naked pictures of yourself on the internet, though. I mean, I'm
not complaining, but. You understand. Yeah. Do you miss home. Yeah. Then
why don't you call your mom. I just don't feel like it right now.

Katana kisses him on the cheek and tells him
he's cute like Bambi, lost without his mother.
Zach tells her to fuck off.

She says, I remember you telling me why you said you didn't want a prosthetic, and I still think it's bullshit. All you're doing is making things harder for yourself. You may think you're special right now and that you're such a goddamn rebel, but when you get older you'll realize it's not that big a deal. Then you'll see how convenient it is.

*

The next day Katana sits across from him
at the table, a spinach salad in front of her.

Have you ever slept with anyone normal, she says. Yeah, he says. Have you. A few times, she says. Okay. It was all right, I had to stand up most of the time. Why. They liked doing it from behind, so I had to leave my prosthetic on and bend over a bit. Oh. We just did that a few times, it wasn't comfortable. Okay. Does that bother you. No.

Zach shakes his head, polishes off a bowl
of Doritos. Katana pours dressing over her salad
and stirs it a little with her fork. She watches him a moment.

Do you like being here, she asks. Why. I wanna know. You've been depressed lately. I've been figuring things out. You've been sitting in front of that computer all the time. So. Are you talking to other women. Is it a crime to talk to other women. If you do it on that website, it's a little suspicious. I'm talking to people like me, or people who wanna talk to me. I wanna talk to you, you just don't give me the chance. You're always busy. Bullshit, she says. Bullshit. Don't give me that. I make time for you, you just never wanna talk to me 'cause you're too caught up in that website and you're too goddamn immature to know how to be in a relationship.

Katana puts down her fork and squeezes
the bridge of her nose. Zach bites his lip,
licking up some of the cheese dust.

I probably knew this before you moved in with me, but I was too happy to have someone like me to really care about it. I didn't think much about the age difference because I thought it'd be easier being with someone who understood what it's like...but. But what. I don't know. I guess it's not as easy as I thought. Are you...do you wanna end this. I don't know. I need to think about it. I like you, but I don't know if you're mature enough for me.

Zach wipes his hands on his jeans, his left hand settling
on the stub. He scrunches up a fold of denim.
Katana leans forward and props her head in her hands.
Zach sees the tattooed wings of the fairy on her forearm
and the knurled elbows of the goblin on her other arm. The way she's
positioned, they seem to be staring each other down.

And I still get the feeling that you haven't told me the truth about your age, she says. Why are you pushing this, Zach says. Because it means something to me, I don't know if I'm committing a crime with you being here or what. It's not a crime. How do I know. You don't tell me, and you haven't told me why you don't tell me. Why not, Zach. Well look where I am. My parents kicked me out and I had to come live with you. What am I supposed to do if you gimme the boot, too. I wouldn't give you the boot. You just said it's a crime. You just said it isn't, she says. Are you saying... No, he says. You're really eighteen. Yes. Okay. Well I'm not twenty-five.

Outside the wind rasps
and curls upwards, rubbing against the window.
The glass shifts a little.

You're not twenty-five, Zach says. No, Katana says. I'm thirty-one. What the fuck. That's why I'm so anxious about your age. I thought if I lessened the difference it'd make it okay. You're almost twice as old as I am. I'm not that old. You're old enough. Does it make a difference for you. Yeah. Do you wanna leave, then. Well. 'Cause where are you gonna stay. You accused me of lying this whole fucking time and now you come out with this. It's fucking gross. I know, and I'm sorry. You're a hypocrite. I know.

Zach sighs and hangs his head. He rubs his eyes and looks out
the window. A bus has stopped out front, its brakes wheezing up
from the street. He takes his crutches and swings himself over.

What're you gonna do, Katana says. I don't know. You gonna call home. I don't
know. Do you want me to call for you. No, don't be stupid, that'd be disgusting.
What's the big deal, I'm still older than you. You lied to me. While accusing me
of lying. I said that I'm sorry. What do you want me to do. I don't know. Are
you not comfortable. I don't know.

Katana stands up, wobbling a little
as her ass has numbed from sitting.

Zach, tell me if I'm wrong, you seem lost lately. Almost like you're homesick.
I'm not homesick. I understand if you wanna go home. I'm not homesick. Then
what is it. I just don't feel comfortable. With me. With you, at home. I don't feel
comfortable anywhere. I almost had another accident at work yesterday. You
remember how I dislocated my arm that one time. Yeah. Well the same thing al-
most happened. The floor in the back, you know, it's all concrete, and there was
a wet spot in the aisle and I slipped on it and almost fell. I grabbed onto one of
the shelves to stop from going all the way. Oh. I'm glad you're okay. Yeah. That
fucking job. I've told my boss how many times that the concrete is always slick
and I can't get a grip on it, and I'm always back there doing inventory and stuff.
I see. Yeah. Like I said, I'm not comfortable anywhere.

Katana raises her eyebrows.
She stretches her arms and starts to say something,
then stops, and starts again.

You know Zach, I was on the internet yesterday, and I saw on the dropdown list
a website that sells prosthetics. Now I wasn't looking at them. Were you. Are
you thinking about getting one. No. You're not. No. Then why was that site on
the computer. I was just.

Zach sighs. Katana nods. Zach pivots and faces her.
It's nothing final, okay. I was just looking. Okay. I'm still not ready. Okay.

Zach bites his lip and squeezes
the foam grips of his crutches.

Why're you smiling at me, he says. Because, she says. You're cute when you
grow up. Whatever.

Zach leans forward on the table. Katana goes to him.
The joints of her prosthetic make a clicking noise.
She puts her hands on his shoulders. Zach sighs.

Are you gonna call home. I guess.

CHANCE

Good Anger

Chance rolls up to his workstation at TramPart Marketing and settles in and starts his computer. He glances down the aisle and notices the narrow wet tracks his wheels left on the floor. The computer boots up; he finds his list of customers and glances at the time zone guide tacked to the wall, Eastern, Mountain, Central. He brings the phone close and starts dialling.

His supervisor comes up to him and waits for him to hang up.

"Okay, thank you, sir." Chance takes off his headset and backs up. "Yeah?"

"You were late again."

"Yeah. I'm still getting used to the bus schedule, and the rain made it hard to get in, 'cause I couldn't get over the puddles."

"Okay, I understand that, but to a point. You gotta start planning ahead or something. You've been late more and more."

"I know, and I'm trying. I'm trying to put things in order and get things going, but it's hard to do that when you're slowed down."

Chance taps the armrests of his wheelchair.

"Okay. Just keep trying. Try to wake up earlier or something."

"I'll try."

The supervisor nods and walks away.

"Fucking asshole." Chance grabs his headset and puts it back on and prepares to make another call.

The day passes idly. Chance eats a bag of carrot sticks and a peanut butter and honey sandwich at his station while most of the others go to the café around the corner. The honey's soaked through the bread; it makes his fingers sticky. He wipes his hands on his jeans and throws the rest of the carrots in the garbage. Then he starts phoning again.

"Good afternoon. Is Mr. Stanley Holland there, please? Mr. Holland of San Antonio, Texas? Hello, sir. My name's Chance, and I'd like to speak to you for a moment about a piece of exercise equipment that virtually guarantees you a healthy body."

"Guarantees a healthy body?"

"Yes, sir."

"Really?"

"Yes."

"That would be wonderful."

"This equipment is—"

"I've been waiting twenty years to hear something like that."

"Okay."

"Yes, twenty years, boy, after I lost my legs and ended up in a goddamn wheel-chair."

"Oh." Chance covers his mouthpiece and whispers, "Fuck. Oh, I'm sorry, sir."

"Guarantees a healthy body. What a bunch of bullshit. Nothing's guaranteed, son."

"I know, sir."

"Is this that equipment they always show on ESPN? With the men with big muscles and flat stomachs and the women that look like them, that sorta deal?"

"I don't know, sir, I don't watch much TV."

"Ah, yeah. You're probably always out running around, aren't you, with your two working legs."

"Actually, that's not true."

"How's that?"

"I'm in a wheelchair, too, sir."

The man is silent for a moment. "What? Really?"

"Yeah."

"You sound like just a young kid. How old are you?"

"Twenty-two."

"What? I thought wheelchairs were only for us old farts. How the hell'd you get in a wheelchair?"

"I was shot."

"Shot? Jesus! By who?"

"A guy."

"What guy?"

"I don't know his name."

"Well, why the hell'd he shoot you?"

"Because he was fat."

"What? That's outrageous."

"I know!"

"Well, did you get him back or what?"

"He's in jail, or will be in jail."

"Christ, son. That's rough. You go to the hospital?"

"Yeah. I was in there for almost a month."

"I was in for three when I lost my legs. I know that's tough business. Tough shit."

"Yeah, it is."

"But I'm sure you'll be okay. I hear some grit in your voice."

"I don't know about that. I feel like I'm angry all the time. You know?"

"Yeah. Yeah, I know." Mr. Holland clears his throat. "But trust me, boy, it gives you grit. Makes you tougher. I know that anger, believe me, and it helped me through everything. It's good to be angry. Then you don't get caught just lying back and doing nothing. Anger makes you want to do something about it."

Chance glances around the stale office and at his computer screen, which has receded into its screensaver.

"Okay," he says.

"Well, good chat, son. What's your name?"

"Chance."

"Chance. Sorry I couldn't buy your equipment, Chance."

"It's okay, sir. Mr. Holland."

"You take care now, hear?"

"I will. Thank you."

Chance hangs up and lowers his headset so that it rests around his neck. He fiddles with his computer mouse and watches the cursor slide across the screen. He drags it up and down, writes out his name in imaginary letters, draws a yin yang. He flings the mouse against the cubicle wall and backs out of his station to go to the washroom, but he forgets his headset is still on, and he's jerked back and his neck strains and he groans and "Fuck!" and all his coworkers shush him as he rips off the headset and throws it back and careens huffily down the aisle.

*

Teresa stands at the door, still holding it open even though Chance has already wheeled into the living room.

"Another hard day at the office?"

"God."

Teresa closes the door and walks up behind Chance and puts her hands on his shoulders. "Carlos again?"

"That fricking asshole. He thinks that I'm late on purpose or something."

"You were late again?"

"I had trouble getting into the bus."

"Didn't the driver help?"

"Yeah, but there was a huge puddle between me and the bus, so I could hardly do anything. We had to manoeuvre around, he had to move the bus just so, and there were people on it, and..."

"Oh."

Chance rubs his eyes. "I hate asking for help."

"I know."

"Makes me feel useless."

"Yeah." Teresa kisses him on the top of the head. "If it'll perk your smile, I got you something."

"You got me something?"

"Yeah. You need to close your eyes."

"What is it?"

"Close them, and wait there."

"Oh, thanks. Where else would I wait?"

"Just shut your eyes."

Chance closes his eyes. A minute later Teresa's footsteps approach and he hears an animal whining. As he opens his eyes Teresa puts a puppy in his lap.

"Something to help get you through everything."

"A puppy?"

"The pick of the litter."

"You got me a puppy?"

"Isn't he cute?"

"What kinda dog is he?"

"He's a malamute. You like him?"

Chance looks the puppy over. "Looks a bit like a sled dog."

"He is a sled dog."

Chance looks at her. "You got a sled dog for a guy in a wheelchair?"

"He'll do you good. He'll make you smile."

"How much was he?"

"Nothing. He was given to me."

"From who?"

"You remember my friend Katie? Her dog had puppies, and she let me pick one out for you." Teresa bends down in front of Chance and rubs the puppy behind its ears. The puppy squeaks. She stands up. "You get to name him."

"What about food and all that?"

"Never mind. What'll you name him?"

"Oh, I don't—ah, dammit!"

Chance lifts up the puppy. A curt whiff of urine rises.

"Take him, please."

Teresa takes the puppy and starts toward the door. "Dammit."

"I gotta go change now."

She takes the leash hanging by the door and puts the puppy down. "Is that the puppy's name?"

"What?"

"Dammit."

Teresa chuckles as she puts on the leash and leads the puppy outside. Chance loosens his belt buckle and unzips his jeans and turns and goes into the bedroom. He pushes up with his right arm and forces down the left leg of his jeans and then the right, pushing up and then pushing them off with both hands. Just as he pulls them off his feet, Teresa comes in with the puppy.

"You okay?"

"Yeah." His underwear is wet, too. He sighs and tugs on the elastic waistband.

"You've been angry a lot lately."

"Yeah."

"I thought this would help."

He grunts and slips the seat of his underwear out. He takes a deep breath and sits back. "How?"

"Give you something different to focus on."

Chance raises his eyebrows, shakes his head. He's sweating and takes a minute before going to the dresser and removing a dry pair of underwear.

"That name feels right," she says.

"What name? Dammit?"

"Yeah."

"Why?"

"Just—with everything. It's funny."

"Everything meaning my anger?"

"Yeah."

Chance pulls on his underwear and pushes up with his arm to slide fully into them.

"I don't know," Teresa says. "It's not healthy to be angry all the time."

"Yeah."

"And what's cuter than a puppy? I thought it'd help you."

"If I name him Dammit, how's that helpful? It'd make me sound angry all the time. 'Come here, Dammit. Go outside, Dammit.' What'll that do?"

The puppy's ears perk and it starts whining and pawing to be let down. Teresa lets it go and it walks up to Chance's chair, sniffing at his feet.

"It just feels right," she says. "It's funny."

Chance reaches down and the puppy licks and bites his fingers.

"He's got those little puppy teeth," he says.

"Yeah."

Chance pats Dammit on the head and ruffles his fur. Dammit jaws at his hand and rears on his hind legs and collapses backwards and tries to tackle the hand.

"Okay, Dammit."

Teresa smiles. "Dammit." She laughs.

"Dammit."

Chance smiles.

THE BUTTERFLY ROOM

HEARING TEST

The few nights that Cherie and I spent together
are dark in my memory. Dark in the way that
she was deaf. Almost all the way. Her cochlear implant
an alien transmitter: two black caps on either side of
her head obscured within the dark curly hedge of her hair.
A red beep. The tattoo on her breast clipped by
her black t-shirt, a slight curve leading down to
something else, something red.

She'd come from Chicoutimi to see me. Why,
I don't clearly remember. To test things. See if we could
stand each other. She was fluent in American Sign Language
and Langue des signes québécoise. My own hands
stammered, lisped, stuttered. I took to writing notes instead.

Though the attraction was there and we were both artists,
she a painter and I a writer, those days and nights
chopped a clean canyon between hearing and listening.
Although she was direct with me everything felt like more
than it was, each word either a massage or a barb.
She hated that I wrote notes. Her fingers whipped like a bullet train,
leaving me awed by their speed but stifled by their blur.
I think I kept waiting for her to say something.

We fucked on the last night. It was swift and tidy.
In bed we were apart and then together. As though
we both said Oh, what the hell? She seized me. Undressed.
Rolled on top. Her pale body a white flag, blue in the dark.
She put me inside her and faced away. I lifted her,
shoved my hips upwards. We both came. Close together,
with loaded sighs. We separated, washed, went back to sleep
apart. No words.

The next day she left. She was supposed to spend two weeks
with me. We lasted three days.
When we'd first met I'd showed her my name sign:
the letter A in sign language made with both fists, then
making drumming motions. When we parted she flicked
the asshole sign at me, suggested it as my new name sign.

It was a test in the end. Little more than the darkness
remains. Though it's a moving darkness:
silent hands cleaving sounds, snapping me to attention.

During a camping trip when I was young, folded up
in my sleeping bag inside the tent by the river, I listened
to my parents' firelight conversations with their friends.
Since I couldn't read their lips, it was all mumbling to me—

yet I noticed how smoothly their voices aligned
with the river, two steady hums rushing parallel along.
Earlier that day my mother and I had been walking
down the trail and we saw an orange bird. It landed

on a branch and began opening and closing its black beak.
My mother knelt down beside me and put her hand on my shoulder.
"Can you hear that?" she said. "It's singing for us."
I stared at the bird, reaching for its song. I heard a soft clicking sound

and asked my mom if that was what it was. Her face was blank for a moment,
then she smiled and said, "That's how you hear it. That's your way.
And you know what? That's all that should matter. That's your own way."

I nestled into the dark cloth belly of my sleeping bag, deep
in my own warmth, and I listened to them talking for a long time,
and I listened to the river gurgling past, settling into my own peace.

Like the child
learning to

navigate irony
my hearing

oscillates between
what's obvious

and what's
obscure

sometimes I
feel the in-between

the living room
of the senses

in which most
of us relax

comforted
by knowing

the difference.
I occupy

a spot in
the corner

never staying long
enough to leave

an imprint in
the cushioned chair.

Now that I'm older, the memories of sounds from my childhood
linger like apparitions: my father's KISS records through
the old Kenwood speakers, Ace Frehley's guitar solos climbing
into higher pitches, swelling past my hearing's orbit
(though I can sense its old distant paths as though by satellite).

Lines from *The Land Before Time* and old *Ghostbusters* episodes are shaped
a certain way; my parents' old phrases murmur on the gravelled periphery
like a familiar river. As I revisit them now, they skid against
the mould my memory has created for them. They sound better
in my memory, thickened with the volume only memory can provide.

It's been a while since my last hearing test.
I arrive after having driven past the university,
where the cows graze in that range of land
cut off from the rest of the campus by a wooden fence.
They stand idly, bent over the familiar stall chewing the hay, slowly
lifting their hooves before setting them back in the same spot.

I meet my audiologist, a smiling open woman.
She asks me a few questions before leading me down the hall
into a small room, dim like a shed.
There's a small table against the wall, on which rests a machine
like a huge graphics calculator: a prominent screen,
grey wires strung out, and earpieces in small plastic containers.
She turns on the machine and the screen lights up. She fits the end of a wire
with an earpiece and nestles it into my ear. A monotone swells up,
like my ear fills with rubber. I swallow and blink against it;
a rigid line forms a small hill on the screen, indicating density, depth.
The same thing for the other ear, then she prints off the screen
and tells me nothing has really changed.

I'm led into a soundproof booth where I sit
amidst wires, metal, beepers. As usual, she goes into the next room
and I watch her through glass. She holds a piece of paper over her face
as she recites certain words to test my range.

She says, Say the word Ate.	Ape.
Say the word Gave.	Dave.
Say the word Rip.	Writ.
Say the word Up.	Ut.
Say the word Peer.	Pew.
Say the word Awe.	Ahh.
Say the word Perch.	Perk.

As she says the words I think of the cows in their pen,
lifting their hooves and settling them back down in the same spot.

But wear hearing aids? In public? Surely
you jest. I hate those bristling rattles like wind
through a tarantula's legs, those tinny aluminum-foil
crinkles, those bad-CB squelches of static,
the uncomfortable closeness of strangers' voices.

> Yes, I wear contact lenses, but not hearing aids.
> It's hard to explain. It's just one of those things,
> like the boy who hates tomatoes and loves pizza sauce.
> You're gonna have to figure it out for yourself.

To be deaf is to have tunnel vision.
The skein of the senses straightens
into crisp focus: a Labrador hones in on
buried rawhide, a child winces from
a stinging hot pepper, Sidney Crosby
zooms in on a loose puck. Not so much
heightened senses as a lack of distraction.

The cure for ADD: wake up your child each morning
with a foghorn. Blare Metallica in his or her ears
instead of reading a bedtime story. Repeat
until he or she keeps asking you to repeat.

When I hear a song for the first time, I always make up the lyrics, compressing the mumbles into what I think I hear, directing them towards what the song title makes me think about.

Then I wait before looking up the real lyrics, at which I'm usually disappointed.

I can ignore you and get away with it.
If I turn my eyes away from you your words
fall uselessly around me. I like it,
actually, turning away towards
more idle, empty spaces and meeting
the images I find there: dense constraints
that thicken the air, anxious glances of fleeting
whimsy, how people toss themselves against
each other. I like how, when I turn away,
I see everything: duplicitous faces,
illusory colours, and ignored graces.
Honestly, I prefer to live this way,
with an excuse to ignore you, and
just enough hearing to know the difference.

THE BUTTERFLY ROOM

Before she enters, Belinda remembers
    what her father told her when she was nine
        and first diagnosed with muscular dystrophy. Her elbows
           had been bent inwards and crossed over her chest, as they are now.
    Her little brother, being little and possessed of the dark
sense of humour that little boys have, told her
    she looked like a vampire sleeping in a coffin.
Her father, an entomologist, wheeled her
    into the alcove looking out on the family garden.
        Sharp greens, sugary pinks and flashing yellows flared in the sun. Her
           father knelt beside her. He said, Belinda, you know what
      you look like. He leaned in and touched her shoulder.
    His dark eyes slipped over his glasses. Her lips pinched.
You look like a butterfly in a cocoon, your limbs
    wrapped in silk, ready to spring out at any moment.

She lingers at the door. Reaches for the knob,
    misses. Her doctor's words from earlier in the day:
      Misunderstood muscle. He'd seemed pleased with his phrasing,
        leaning back with his file in front of him. She manoeuvres her chair,
      taking her time aligning herself. She reaches and settles
her hand on the knob, lets the metal's coolness radiate
throughout her palm. On the door is a wooden slate.
    The room's title's burned into it in deep black
      block letters. She can almost hear
  the flutters. She twists the knob and pushes in
      the door. A screen of dark netting. The humid air of a greenhouse.
    A hint of the old concrete in the solidity of the ground.
This used to be the garage. The smell of stale grass
    clippings and spilled oil has been replaced by
the scent of minced black earth and green bloom.

Her brother loves monsters. Just down the hall
　　on his bedroom door is a portrait of Nosferatu,
　　　　the bald vampire with his arms crossed over his chest,
　　　　　　his eyes blazing. His nails, long and predatory, could claw through
　　　　concrete. She asked him to take it down, but he　.
　　persisted, as little boys do. Inside his room, from
the brief glimpses he's allowed her, the walls
　　are glossy with monsters: bent faces, speckled scales,
spackles of blood flashing white in the sunlight drifting in
　　from the blinds. He's at that age, her father said, where he's obsessed
　with strange things. He was working at his desk
　　at the time, gripping a large beetle with the tweezers.
I'm sure his fascination will dwindle off, he said.

She shuts the door. A few of them wait for her,
　　resting on the netting. With as much care as she can
　　　　manage she negotiates her way through the screen's
　　　　　　opening, a long slit in the middle, nudging forward the joystick
　　　　on her chair. One of them, a leopard-spotted Painted Lady,
　　skips off the netting and whisks on into the room.
The others hold their ground, sinking into their
six-legged stances. Sunlight floods the room.
　　　A Japanese maple rests in the middle, its branches
　　　　spreading along the vaulted glass ceiling. She steers her chair down
　　　the earthen path and comes to rest underneath the tree.
　Shadows undulate on the ground. She glances up. Sighs.
Chew-holes through the maple's leaves. Caterpillars speckled
　and dark pock the leaves and the bark. White and grey cocoons
　　abound. The air is moist, enveloping. She makes a noise, a call
　　　　just loud enough to stir. She listens closely for the light whirr of wing beats,
　　sees the frolicking ochre, the flapping purple, the whirling yellow,
　the Purple-Shot, the Black-veined White, the Apollo, the Monarch,
the Mojave Checkerspot, the Danube Clouded Yellow. Her favourite
　is the Purple-edged, its wings billowing out like a cloak. She loves
　　how some of them look exactly like their names and how some of them

look nothing like their names. In this room she feels like Belinda, her arms curled as if in metamorphic slumber, the tiny fibrous legs of her peers stirring the lightest nerves of her skin; to her, the itch of transformation.

NOTES ON THE POEMS

"Deaf Speech": The lines from "Eye of the Tiger" are from Survivor's album of the same name, released via the Scotti Brothers label in 1982. Mr. Dedalus appears courtesy of James Joyce's *A Portrait of the Artist as a Young Man* (1916). Mr. Bloom and Mr. Mulligan originally arose in 1922's *Ulysses*. The "Dieuf and Domb" line is from *Finnegans Wake* (1939), which inspired Dance of Tongues as well as the use of the New Zealand haka, which appears in Joyce's final novel in a slightly altered form. As mentioned, the haka is a traditional dance performed by the Maori people of New Zealand and popularized by the All-Blacks rugby team.

A number of sources were consulted for the "Alberta Provincial Training School for Mental Defectives" sequence. Especially helpful were the 1996 film *The Sterilization of Leilani Muir* and Heather Pringle's article "Alberta Barren: The Mannings and forced sterilization in Canada," which appeared in *Saturday Night Magazine* in June 1997. The court excerpts are from the famed Leilani Muir sterilization trial. The full court summary is available online.

ACKNOWLEDGEMENTS

First to my family: Mum, Dad and Taylor. Collectively you three helped form my conscience, which is everything to a writer. Thank you and love you.

Two extraordinary teachers, Ian Kluge and Kathy Sawatsky, gave me the ol' nudge-nudge towards writing.

Vici Johnstone saw merit in something different and was bold enough to publish it. Thank you so much; I will always be grateful.

The superbly talented Laura Ferguson allowed us to use her painting for the cover.

Through her photography wizardry, Kristen Hergott somehow made me look palatable for the author photograph.

Robert Budde and Ken Belford, purveyors of northern BC, advised me throughout the administrative process, ensuring I didn't walk into publishing uninformed.

Anne Simpson, former Writer in Residence at the Saskatoon Public Library, was gracious, insightful and generous with her time.

Jordan Scott offered encouragement and commentary on the manuscript. Thank you.

The sonnet at the end of "Hearing Test" is for Elizabeth Bachinsky, whose work prompted me towards the sonnet form.

Taylor Leedahl, Lisa Johnson, Charles Hamilton and Stephen Rutherford of the Saskatoon Tonight it's Poetry crew helped me find an audience. Many of these poems were first read and tested before the TIP crowd.

Special thanks to my editor Joe Denham, a.k.a. "Chief," the personal trainer who whipped this book into shape by shedding fat and tightening muscle.

Finally, to my darling wench, Debbie. Love you with everything I have. "Earth angel, earth angel..."

About the author

ADAM POTTLE was born in Kamloops, BC, in 1984, and grew up in Ashcroft, Kitimat and Prince George. His first chapbook, *Bereft*, co-won the 2008 Barry McKinnon Chapbook Prize. He currently lives in Saskatoon, where he is pursuing a doctoral degree in English Literature. *Beautiful Mutants* is his first full-length book.

About the artist

LAURA FERGUSON is a New York artist whose drawings, prints, and artist's books have been widely exhibited in galleries and museums in New York and around the United States, including the Museum of Science in Boston, the National Museum of Health and Medicine in Washington, DC, and the Chicago Cultural Center. Her work is represented in the collections of the National Library of Medicine and the American Academy of Orthopaedic Surgeons. In 2008 she became Artist in Residence at the NYU School of Medicine, where she teaches anatomy drawing to medical students and uses the 3D Imaging Lab and the Anatomy Lab as sources for the anatomical imagery in her own art.

ARTIST STATEMENT

My work is all about the body. Being both artist and model allows me to work from the inside out—to convey the feeling of inhabiting inner space, and the ways that personal identity and even consciousness are rooted in physical experience. I use drawing to portray the body's visceral physicality, its inherent beauty, uniqueness, and visual complexity, and its connection to the processes and patterns of nature. My drawings are intimate and sensual but at the same time strongly grounded in science: in an understanding of anatomy and physiology and specifically in medical images of my own body made for the purpose of art.

MORE POETRY FROM CAITLIN PRESS

And See What Happens, Ursula Vaira
88 pp, pb, ISBN 978-1-894759-58-8, $16.95

In her first book of poetry, Ursula Vaira captures the rugged and challenging beauty of the West Coast landscape in three poignant stories. Lorna Crozier has called these poems "talismans of grace, beauty and healing." In *And See What Happens,* Ursula Vaira writes the poetry of three transformative journeys in British Columbia's wilderness.

Unfurled: Collected Poetry from Northern BC Women, edited by Debbie Keahey
208 pp, pb, ISBN 978-1-894759-52-6, $22.95

Ambulance lights flash as a baby is born on a busy city street, pine beetles paint forests a palette of new colours, a young boy faces a watery death under the ice of a frozen lake, and a mother stands in a bathtub at midnight wearing only her gumboots. In this anthology of new writing, women poets from Northern BC share their refreshing, intriguing, mystical and sometimes mythical insights into rural and urban life.

Walk Myself Home: An Anthology to End Violence Against Women, edited by Andrea Routley
184 pp, pb, ISBN 978-1-894759-51-9, $22.95

There is an epidemic of violence against women in Canada and the world. For many women physical and sexual assault, or the threat of such violence, is a daily reality. *Walk Myself Home* is an anthology of poetry, fiction, nonfiction and oral interviews on the subject of violence against women including contributions by Kate Braid, Yasuko Thahn and Susan Musgrave.